Mendip Country

by

JILLIAN POWELL

with photographs by

JULIA DAVEY

BOSSINEY BOOKS

First published in 1987 by
Bossiney Books
St Teath, Bodmin, Cornwall.

Typeset, Printed and Bound by
Clowes Book Printers
St Columb, Cornwall.

Plate Acknowledgments
Front Cover by Rosemary and Michael Clinch.

Pages 20-23 by courtesy of Austin Wookey;
rephotographed by Julia Davey.

Page 34 by courtesy of Cheddar Caves.

All other photographs by Julia Davey.

CONTENTS

About the Author and the book

Jillian Powell was educated at Norwich High School and Newnham College, Cambridge, where she was awarded Double First Class Honours in English. After leaving Cambridge, she went on to study the History of Art at the Courtauld Institute, London. She now divides her time between London and the country, working as a freelance writer and teaching English and Art History. She is currently working on a book on nineteenth-century watercolours.

Early in 1985, Jillian Powell made her debut for Bossiney, contributing two excellent chapters in *Westcountry Mysteries,* introduced by Colin Wilson: one on the Beast of Exmoor, the other on the disappearance of Genette Tate.

Later in 1985 Jillian Powell, accompanied by photographer Julia Davey, explored *The Quantocks.* Their sensitive combination of words and pictures — all especially commissioned for the book — produced a delightful portrait of the area.

Her Bossiney work also includes a chapter on churches and inns of Bristol in the book *People & Places in Bristol* which is introduced by best-selling novelist E.V. Thompson.

Here in *Mendip Country* Jillian Powell, again with photographer Julia Davey, explores these famous Westcountry hills which stretch for some twenty miles. 'These hills are rife with history and legend,' the author reflects. '...the rich variety of the Mendip countryside is matched by its towns and villages.'

Many of the best of regional books happily combine the personality of the writer with the characteristics of the area — the response of one to the other — and this is a delightful example of that happy combination. Here, too, fine photographs underline both the quality of the places and the people — and the book itself.

RIGHT *Author, Jillian Powell*

Mendip Country

Mendip is many places, from deep underground caverns to turfy heathered uplands; from Wells with its exuberant Gothic Cathedral and moated Bishop's Palace to the natural drama of the Cheddar Gorge. The hills themselves stretch for about twenty miles, running south-eastwards from the headland of Brean Down in the Bristol Channel, haunt of the raven and the peregrine falcon, to the bustling market town of Frome. They rise from flat plains to the highest point of 1068 feet at Black Down, and from here the trig stone looks west to Brean Down and the uninhabited, whale-backed island of Steep Holm, and east over the silvery reservoirs of Blagdon and the Chew Valley.

The turfy paths on this tableland are cleft by horseshoes, for this is a favourite place for riders and for walkers or whortleberry pickers who have climbed the half mile from the top of Burrington Combe. It is here that you get a sense of the limestone ridge of Mendip curving away south-eastwards — site of Iron Age hill forts and the ancient Priddy sheep fair — where beacons were lit at the time of the Armada and during the Napoleonic Wars.

These hills are rife with history and legend, from the Prehistoric earthworks at Banwell and the Priddy Nine Barrows, to mystic Glastonbury down on the Somerset Levels, birthplace of the State, where the Kings of Wessex, Arthur and Alfred, set up their governments. In Saxon and early Medieval times, Mendip land was a Royal Hunting Forest for the tall red deer; there is a story that in 941 King Edmund narrowly escaped death when his hounds chased a stag over the cliffs at Cheddar in thick fog.

The Romans mined lead on Mendip; pigs of lead and coins from the reigns of successive Roman Emperors have been found, and from Winscombe in the west to Whatley in the east, there are tracts of 'gruffy ground', land made rough and hummocky by the circular 'gruffs' or mining shafts.

The gruffy ground around Charterhouse and Priddy has become a popular place for Sunday walkers. Here, the flues and the buddles — where the ore was refined — of the Victorian smelting works can still be clearly seen, while the settling ponds are now

RIGHT *The Author at Aveline's Hole, Burrington Combe on the Mendips*

6

ABOVE *A dialogue of trees beneath the Ammerdown Tower in the parish of Kilmersdon*

rich wildlife habitats, thick with bullrushes and harbouring rare plants like the Alpine Penny-Cress. It is a dramatic landscape in places, sliced by the Roman 'rakes' or mine workings, beside the site of the miners' settlement known as 'Bleak House'.

The very stones of Mendip are linked with legend, like the Wimblestone near Shipham, which is said to conceal a hoard of gold and to dance across the fields at night. Just north of the hills, towards Bristol, are the three circles of standing stones at Stanton Drew, whose legend is that they were wedding guests turned to stone by the devil, disguised as a fiddler, as their punishment for drinking and dancing on into the Sabbath.

It is the limestone of Mendip which has shaped the hills with their deep craggy gorges, broken uplands and labyrinthine underground caverns and streams. Where rivers have penetrated joints in the stone, fields are pocked with 'swallet holes', source of the streams which wind underground through caves once home to Stone Age man, to re-emerge in springs at the foot of the hills.

It is limestone, too, which, like Norfolk flint or Cornish granite, gives the landscape its character. Hard and resistant to weathering, limestone scars the valley sides and straddles the fields in dry stone walls, or appears, patterned with lichens, in the walls of houses or churches, like the Methodist Chapel at Leigh-on-Mendip. In Mendip buildings, the stone of the hills is everywhere evident, from the hewn white Doulting stone of Wells Cathedral, to the grey-etched lias of the millworkers' cottages at Midsomer Norton and Radstock. At Burrington, church and cottages are built in the local dolomitic conglomerate flecked with sand, white, grey and russet, which seams the hills, while at Blagdon, the church tower takes its rosy colouring from the old red sandstone of the rounded uplands.

Stone has long been one of Mendip's major resources, but today quarrying has become a controversial issue, with the local amenity organisation, the Mendip Society, strongly opposed to the expansion of the limestone quarries with their attendant noise, dust and heavy haulage. While the roadstone companies maintain that they are taking increasing care to minimise problems, with tree-screening of quarries and afforestation of waste tips, the Society argues that with much of Mendip an Area of Outstanding Natural Beauty, the hills should be protected for recreation and leisure, as well as for agricultural purposes. The stone of Mendip, they affirm, has not only a commercial, but a precious landscape

BELOW *Gathering whortleberries on Black Down, a favourite place for riders and walkers*

and amenity value, and while Mendip may be the nearest source of limestone aggregate to the south-east, it is also the nearest source of wild, limestone upland — a vanishing resource.

Over the centuries, man has culled Mendip not only of stone, but of the mineral ores, lead, calamine, iron, copper and coal, in its rich substratum. The low riverside levels provided peat for fuel — now used for horticultural purposes — and osiers for the basket makers. Local fullers earth, combined with a damp atmosphere and clean, fast flowing streams, encouraged the growth of the cloth industry, which survived, on a small scale, into the nineteenth century. (In 1857, the industry made 'superior cloth' for the Emperor of Russia, and kerseymere for the harems of the Sultan of Constantinople.) Towns and villages in the east were famous for the quality of their broadcloth, those in the south for their knitted goods.

The same rivers spawned grist mills and paper mills, ironworks and breweries. The majority have long since gone, but evocative ruins of the ironworks survive near Mells, and at Wookey the paper mill is working once again, under the auspices of Madame Tussaud's, providing quality handmade papers for artists and draughtsmen, and tours for the visitors flocking to the caves at Wookey Hole.

RIGHT *Conversation piece at Frome Market*

BELOW *Banwell Churchyard. St Andrew's Church is known as the 'Cathedral of the Mendips'*

Some of Mendip's traditional industries and family firms survive, too, as at Street, headquarters of Clarks Shoes, and at Shepton Mallet, home to the cider and perry makers Showerings. But farming remains Mendip's main industry. Traditionally, the uplands are sheep country, with dairy herds for the local Cheddar cheese kept on the fertile lower slopes and valleys. Market gardening flourishes on these sheltered slopes, with barley, early potatoes, strawberries and anemones grown in the rich red loam near Axbridge.

A large proportion of the hills is now enclosed and farmed, but there are still wild and secret places on the uplands, haunt of the walker and the painter, and the countryside harbours a rich variety of wildlife. There are badgers and foxes in the combes, lizards and adders on the hills, and bats in the caves. Rare dragonflies skim the surface of hilltop dew ponds, and some rare plants like the hawkweed mossy saxifrage still grow on the rock ledges in the gorges, where wrens and jackdaws nest.

The rich variety of the Mendip countryside is matched by its towns and villages, from the isolated hilltop village of Priddy with its ancient sheep fair symbolised by the hurdle-stack on the Green, to Frome with its bustling Wednesday cattle market and picturesque Cheap Street, whose flower-decked, timber-framed shops run either side of a pavement refreshed by a central leat.

There are picturesque villages, like Nunney, with its moated castle ruins, and dour little mining towns like Coleford, with its rubble-built cottages, Methodist Chapel and steep, narrow streets.

At Nunney, when the Fussell's ironworks closed towards the end of the nineteenth century, the lane known as Iron Mills became plain 'Mill Lane'. Now, the family who live at Nunney Court, once the home of the Fussell family, keep donkeys in the field by the lane, and to the locals it has become 'Donkey Lane' — a reminder that Mendip history lives with its people — especially those who have lived and worked on Mendip all their lives, like Austin Wookey.

RIGHT *The ruins of Nunney Castle*

OVERLEAF *Skies over Black Down*

Mendip in the Old Days
RECOLLECTIONS OF AUSTIN WOOKEY

Born in Widcombe in 1902, Austin Wookey left school at West Harptree at the age of fourteen, to work as a 'vermin trapper' or gamekeeper on the local estates of Eastwood Manor and, later, Green Ore. He can still remember rearing partridges on ants' eggs, catching rabbits in the snow, and watching by night for the poachers who would come out with their 'long nets' when the rabbits were feeding in the woods.

'All my young days before I left school I was out with the guns shooting,' Austin recalls. 'My father, a coachman, was a great shot.' For Austin, the countryside around his trim bungalow at Coley, where he has spent all his married life, is rich with memories.

He remembers, as 'a *mischieful* boy' of eleven, riding around the Mendip lanes in pony and trap to read the meters for Henry Tyte, charge hand for the Bristol Waterworks at Litton reservoir, who could 'call his workmen a mile away with his strong voice'. When they saw a man lying drunk in the hedges, Henry would get Austin to cut a hazel stick about a foot long, split it like a peg, and 'put the barnacles' on the drunken man's nose, making a hasty escape just as the man woke up!

'I was full of mischief,' Austin smiles. 'I remember the old steam engine drivers teaching me to get steam up in an old Stanley steam car abandoned in the brambles at Coley Mill...I used to drive the mile up the road to Widcombe, turn round, and get back just as the steam ran out. They used to have fun alive seeing me drive that car!'

Austin still has the brass lamps and the horn from the car, which belonged to Edward Masters, last owner of Coley Mill, who is pictured here taking delivery of a steam engine from the Harrises Motor Works at Chewton Mendip, to fetch corn from the docks at Avonmouth. Coley Mill has long since gone, but Austin recalls the days when gleaners would take grist to the mill to make the flour for 'crock cakes' — prised from the 'crock' in which a stew was cooked.

He can still tell many stories of the early days of steam, too, like the time Mr Harris took the village children to Weston, on their

RIGHT Austin Wookey has lived and worked on Mendip all his life

Methodist Chapel outing, in his brand new steam wagon — and they returned with their faces black with soot! Then there was the farmer, who woke his wife at 6 a.m., crying 'Wake up! We've been asleep for years and they've been and built a railway!' as the first steam engine on Mendip roads puffed and chugged into view.

Austin's work on the local estates brought him into contact with men like Commander Bayntun Hippisley of Ston Easton, a frequent guest at shooting parties held on the Eastwood Manor and Harptree Court estates. A great inventor, even at the age of 90 he would stay up late in his workshop, 'too busy to stop and have a meal, his wife used to say'. He is seen here on a practice run for one of his inventions, a fire engine for the Ston Easton estate.

For power on the estate, a horse-drawn engine was used, and Austin recalls the story of the engine being hauled up to Pen Hill on the night of Queen Victoria's Jubilee in 1887, to send beams from carbon arc lamps across the sky in every direction. When nineteen year-old Charlie Wookey (no relation) saw the lights, he ran all the way home, bursting in on his mother and father and bolting the door behind him — in his belief that the end of the world had come!

'People have been driven crazy by superstition,' Austin smiles. 'I remember seeing Halley's comet when I was a boy in 1910. It was a beautiful night, and you could see the edge of the Mendip hills

BELOW *Edward Masters taking delivery of his new steam engine from Bill Uphill*

ABOVE *Practice run for the fire engine at Ston Easton*

against the skyline. There was about a foot between the tail of the comet and the hills. Well, the wife of one of the Keepers, who lived at Widcombe, came knocking at my mother's door in a real frenzy. "When that tail touches the hills," she cried, "the world is going to blow up!"'

With his dark hair, the 'Spaniard' Austin was much in demand for crossing the threshold on New Year's Eve, to bring good luck, but he has never had much time for superstition.

'As a boy, I used to be warned to keep away from the old lady living at the Squatter's House just by here. They said she'd turn you into a pig...but she was a dear old soul!'

Austin remembers many of the characters of Mendip in the old days: Dicky Adams, who used to sing for Cecil Sharp in the Castle of Comfort; 'Nommie' the snail man, whom Austin, when he was a boy, used to help collect Mendip snails, or 'wall-fish' from nooks in the walls; and Charlie Fry, 'the funniest character I've ever met'. Austin remembers meeting Charlie one day on his way down from milking cows in the field, his yoke and buckets over his shoulders.

'He was in a bit of a panic because he realised he had forgotten to strain the milk, as was required by the law.' Austin watched in horror as Charlie peeled off his threadbare old sweater, and strained the milk through that!

Like Coley Mill and Charlie Fry, many of the people and places of Old Mendip are now consigned to early photographs and to

21

memory. Yet all around him, in the Mendip countryside, Austin sees clues to its history and legend. On Smithem's Hill, by a dewpond veiled with dragonflies, is the last surviving lead mine chimney on Mendip. Austin remembers the rough stone *round houses* used by mining families — a miner was allocated a plot of land measuring the distance he could throw a hack — and the old man who was paid sixpence a day for taking 'pigs' of lead over Mendip from Charterhouse to Uphill, on horsedrawn sleighs.

It was up on Smithem's Hill, in a corner of the Francis Plantation, that the 'Harptree Hoard' of almost 1500 Roman coins with a signet ring and silver ingots was discovered in July 1887 by William Currell, who was digging for water during an exceptionally dry summer. Currell carried the treasure, wrapped in a red cotton handkerchief, down to the Kettlewells at Harptree Court. Some of the coins were given away as gifts — the rarer ones are in the British Museum.

It was the Kettlewell family of East Harptree, who built the village theatre, now the village hall, where Austin remembers seeing the magic lantern shows, and, to commemorate Queen Victoria's Diamond Jubilee, installed the village clock, its message, *Time flies: Don't Delay,* a reminder of the changes in village life on Mendip, since the old days.

BELOW *Coachman Seeward Heal, a former ostler at Chewton Mendip*

RIGHT *Charlie Fry*

LEFT *Austin Wookey with the author by the lead chimney on Smithem's Hill*

Mendip Today:
Towns and Villages

Nestling in the hollows and valleys of Mendip are villages and market towns which, with their mellow local stone and ancient church towers, retain an old fashioned charm. On the north-east side of the hills is the ancient village of Compton Martin, with its reddish stone and whitewashed barns and cottages, green village pump and white ducks on the pond overlooked by the Post Office Stores.

Compton Martin

There is now a public garden where the village sheep dip was, and teazels no longer carpet the ground here as they did when the cloth mills were flourishing, but the little Norman church of St Michael stands intact, with its sturdy round pillars, broad Norman arches and sixteenth century tower. Swallows nest in the church porch, and inside, on the south side of the nave, is the 'cable' or twisted pillar, perhaps a survivor of an earlier chantry on this site, though long reputed to have been a test piece for apprentice stone masons.

Dinder

Directly across the hills, on the southern flanks east of Wells, is Dinder. Here, sheep graze by the fifteenth century church, and a row of gabled cottages, their red tiled roofs decorated with terracotta dragons, look over Dinder water, green with algae, to the undulating hills beyond. There are two fine houses here, Shercombe and Dinder, both built in the nineteenth century, while at Mells, on the eastern fringes of Mendip, and once an eastern outpost of the Glastonbury estate, the early Elizabethan manor has been home to the Horner family for generations.

Mells

Mells, said to be the 'plum' that (little Jack) Horner, the Abbey's bailiff in the sixteenth century, chose for himself, is a picture-book village with its Medieval street, planned by Abbot Selwood, and the old Talbot Inn with its flagged court yard and dove holes in the eaves. From the churchyard, an avenue of clipped yew leads to the fields beyond, giving views over the gabled manor house — where Charles I slept in 1644, during the Civil War — and the church, built circa 1500, with its 100 foot tower.

Here are the tombs of war poet Siegfried Sassoon — who wished to be buried near the grave of priest and scholar Ronald

Knox who lies here — and of the Horner family, their tombstones designed by Edwin Lutyens. More of his work may be seen inside the church, in the plinth for the bronze equestrian statue by Munnings in the Horner Chapel, to Edward Horner, last male heir to the estate, who died in France in the Great War. Lighting the chapel, is a stained glass window of St Francis feeding the birds and fishes, by William Nicholson, portrait painter and father of artist Ben Nicholson.

In the valley below Mells are the derelict cottages and ivy-covered ruins of the ironworks founded in the eighteenth century, and developed in the nineteenth century by the Fussell family. This once thriving industry began to decline in the 1870s, and today it is quarrying which dominates the Mells area, with A.R.C.'s Whatley quarry, one of Mendip's largest roadstone quarries, undergoing extensive redevelopment.

As demands for roadstone aggregates increase, particularly in the south-east, quarrying keeps pace with advanced new machinery, massive production targets (it is forecast that Whatley

Axbridge

will have a production capacity of up to 10 million tonnes per year) and increased rail and road transport. Cheek by jowl with historic villages like Mells and Nunney, the quarries grow, their vast lunar landscapes fringed by green fields and pinnacled church towers: modern industry in striking contrast with the past.

In the bustling Medieval market town of Axbridge, past and present mingle pleasantly with bookshops, tearooms and grocer's clustering around the ancient paved market place and along the narrow streets of half-timbered and colour-washed houses. A fortified 'burh' since Saxon times, when its market supplied the Royal Palace at Cheddar, Axbridge prospered on wool from Mendip sheep in the Middle Ages. This Medieval prosperity is reflected in its fine gabled and halftimbered houses, and in the Perpendicular church of St John the Baptist, built on thirteenth century foundations.

The church stands poised above the market square, the pierced parapets and pinnacles of its mellow 'Cheddar-type' tower seen against the steep curve of Mendip to the north. Inside, unexpected splashes of colour are provided by the striking, seventeenth century painted tomb of Anne Prowse, bonneted in black and white, and surrounded by winged cherub heads, and by the seventeenth century plasterwork ceiling painted in white on blue

and embossed in red and gold, by local craftsman George Drayton, for the sum of ten guineas.

Across the square, where once a fifteenth century market cross and village stocks stood, are more buildings of interest: fifteenth century almshouses now restored as a restaurant, their mullions freshly carved, their curving pantiles screening a fine Medieval timber roof; the Medieval House, its thick black timbers like the sweep of a calligrapher's brush, and King John's Hunting Lodge, a late Medieval merchant's house, now owned by the National Trust and run as a museum of local history.

The lodge may owe its name — an anachronism since it was built some 300 years after King John — to the days when it was run as the King's Head ale-house in the seventeenth and eighteenth centuries, when, perhaps, it was embellished with the carved and painted head which looks down over the square. But, with its crooked bleached timbers, studded oak doors, and tales of a White Lady and a phantom cat, the lodge is ripe for legend. Standing on the corner of the market place and the High Street, it looks out over the square where markets have been held since Saxon times, and fairs since the thirteenth century: scene of processions, festivals, bull baiting and cock fighting — and still presided over today on special occasions by Axbridge's town crier.

Tucked under the steps leading to the church, behind Medieval chamfered arches shaded with pink valerian, are the town wells, whose source is on the Mendip hills, and where, in 1679, a writer complained that 'divers inhabitants doe frequently wash and swele cloths, bullocks bellys, cabbage and other things within the rayles'. Opposite, is the Regency Town Hall, a graceful addition to the square which in summer, with its window boxes and hanging baskets bright with lobelia and petunias, has an old world charm.

Cheddar

A mile and a half away, along the southern flank of Mendip, is Cheddar, famed for the three Cs: 'caves, cliffs and cheese'. Like Axbridge, Cheddar was an ancient settlement, and the outline of its Saxon palace, along with the thirteenth century Chapel of St Columbanus, may be seen in the grounds of the Kings of Wessex School. Cheddar's history, as a Royal manor until it was sold by King John in 1204, later passing to the See of Bath and Wells, is reflected in the Perpendicular church of St Andrew, where kings' and bishops' heads alternate on the corbels supporting the timbers of the moulded and painted oak ceiling.

The church was built between 1380 and 1480, when Cheddar was a busy wool centre, and at the heart of the village, where several roads radiate, is the fifteenth century preaching cross where once travellers and merchants could pay rent to display their wares. A short walk away is the whitewashed cottage where, in 1789, with the support of William Wilberforce and the banker Thornton, Hannah More set up her first school, having

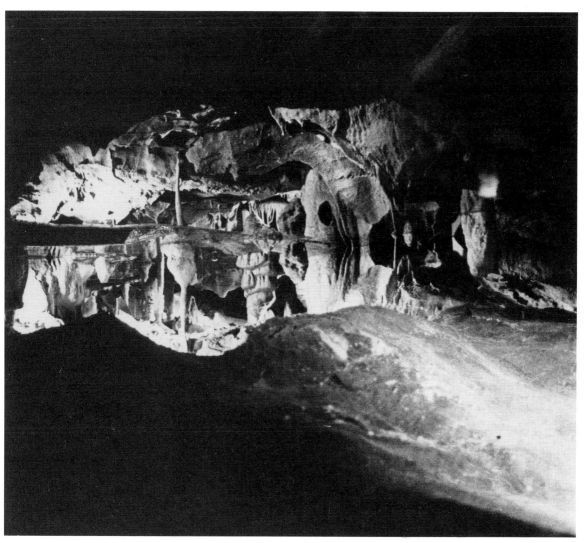

ABOVE AND LEFT *Two magnificent formations on view in Gough's Cave at Cheddar*

ABOVE *St Andrew's Church at Cheddar*

RIGHT *Burrington Combe*

commented on Cheddar:

'We saw but one Bible in all the parish...and that was used to prop up a flowerpot.'

But despite these landmarks, the Gorge and the Caves remain Cheddar's chief attractions. The entrances to the caves can be found at the foot of the gorge, surrounded by a huddle of tourist attractions: tropical house and butterfly centre, souvenir shops, pottery, burger bars and hot dog stalls. But once inside, the bustle of modern tourism dissipates, in a world of echoing tunnels, grottoes shimmering with glassy stalactites and stalagmites, and shadowy caverns, haunt of the horseshoe bat.

The larger of the caves is Gough's, which winds underground for half a mile deep beneath Mendip through spectacular chambers carved by the river Yeo, where stalactites cascade like frozen waterfalls, and stalagmites cluster, glimmering under white light with mineral ores — grey lead, red iron-oxide, green copper carbonate.

Richard Cox Gough began digging here at the end of a short cave, in 1890, opening the way through to the great staircase of stalagmite basins known as the Fonts, and by stages on through to the two great chambers of St Paul's, and King Solomon's Temple, discovered in 1898. While displays in the cave remind one of caving conditions when explorers wore hats stuffed with newspapers and stiffened with tar, and carried no light but candles or oil lamps, visitors today descend easily along the spacious, sloping tunnel, passing the Fonts cascading with water to their right, and, to their left, the Skeleton Pit, where, during excavations in 1903, the skeleton of Cheddar Man, some 10,000 years old, was found.

A recorded commentary points out features of interest: the scalloping, or 'beaten copper' effect on cave ceilings, formed by tiny eddy currents in the underground river; the hart's tongue fern clustering around the light and warmth of the lamps; the constant temperature of eleven degrees centigrade.

Stalagmites and stalactites are given evocative names: the Ring o' Bells, the organ pipes of Solomon's Temple, Niagara in Winter, the Swiss Village. In St Paul's Chamber, beneath a lofty cavern ringed with a ledge reminiscent of the Whispering Gallery in the Cathedral, a cascade of flowstone descends 70 feet to the exquisite Aladdin's Cave, glimpsed between boulders, its fairy-like formations mirrored in a still pool of water. Through, in King Solomon's Temple, where guides sometimes extinguish the lights, allowing 'dawn' to break slowly over the grottoes, a passage leads to the boulder-strewn chamber where blue light, the only coloured light used in the caves, casts a haunting shadow of a black cat. Beyond, through dark and narrow passages, and below a 40 foot sheer drop, is the chamber where, in 1966, a man spent a record 130 days alone.

While Gough's Cave is spacious and spectacular, Cox's, discovered in 1837 by George Cox when he was quarrying limestone near his water mill, is smaller, but exquisite. With their 'scalloping', rounded hollows and high fissures, these caves are, like Gough's, an abandoned river channel. In the Transformation Grotto, visitors pass through a tunnel hollowed out *beneath* delicate curtains of stalactite and fragile stalagmite pillars tinted with red iron oxide, blue manganese and green algae. Beyond are imitative formations: the Speaker's mace and staff, a redwood tree trunk, the three stalactites called the Peal of Bells, while in the Rainbow Room, guides point out a rhinoceros, a sarcophagus, a monkey climbing a tree.

Emerging from this magical underground world into daylight, visitors can climb the 274 steps of Jacob's Ladder, scaling the side of the Gorge, to the tower which gives panoramic views over the Mendip farmland and the bowl of the Cheddar Reservoir — on a clear day as far as the Quantocks and Exmoor. To the west, is the Cheddar Gorge itself, described by twelfth century Chronicler Henry of Huntingdon as one of the four wonders of England, its 400 foot cliffs cutting into the Mendip Hills for two miles. In the past, geologists have attributed the Gorge to the effects of earthquake, sea erosion, or to the collapse of a mammoth cave; it is now believed to have been cut by a river, the ground eroding in two stages. Nature trails lead from the Gorge to the top of the cliffs, past crags and pinnacles of rock festooned with ivy and fern, and harbouring a rich variety of flora including the now rare Cheddar pink, a favourite with the Victorians on account of its sweet smell.

Charterhouse and Priddy

A drive through the Gorge leads up onto Mendip, the road branching one way to Charterhouse, the other to Priddy. 800 feet above sea level, the stern little chapel of St Hugh's, Charterhouse, stands among windy hills on a slight swell of land overlooking the scrub and hummocky ground of the lead mine workings. Named after St Hugh of Witham Abbey, which had a cell for the monks here, the chapel, a former meeting room for the lead miners, was converted into a church in 1908, by the Reverend Menzies Lambrick. Under the supervision of W. D. Caroe, an inventive Arts and Crafts Gothicist, the interior was transformed — the rich detail of its carved oak and Victorian furnishings belied by the chapel's austere, blind-eyed exterior.

St Hugh's is a prominent landmark for walkers roaming over the gruffy ground at Charterhouse, now an Ancient Monument of Industrial Landscape. With its high levels of lead, zinc and cadmium, the land here has been mined for centuries, perhaps even in Prehistoric times. The Romans began mining lead here circa 50 AD, and it is possible to see the Roman rakes, or mine workings, and the site of the miners' settlement. But much of the surface we see today was created in the nineteenth century, when

On the sign in the image:

PRIDDY FAIR

5,000 SHEEP

FIS

ABOVE *The Priddy Fair, showing the hurdle stack*

earlier debris was refined and resmelted to extract further lead. Walkers can see the circular 'buddles' where ore was refined, the condenser flues, for smelting, the heaps of glossy black slag which crunch underfoot, and the settling ponds, fringed with reeds and bullrushes, which are now havens for wildlife.

Like Charterhouse, the village of Priddy, a Medieval market centre where Mendip wool was collected for clothiers down in the valleys, is situated high on Mendip. From its spacious churchyard, the thirteenth century church looks down over the grey, slate-roofed cottages and barns clustered around the triangular green where, every August, on the Wednesday nearest the 21st, the Priddy Sheep Fair is held.

Legend has it that the plague drove the fair here from Wells in 1348 — though the heavy tolls charged in that city may have been the reason — and that the fair will return here each year, so long as the symbolic thatched hurdle stack is standing on the green. Bleak and windswept in winter, Priddy is transformed by the summer crowds flocking to the fair. Farmers from all over Mendip, and from

ABOVE *The Witch of Wookey in the Great Cave*

as far away as Bristol and Bath, converge for the sales of sheep and farm implements which begin at 11 a.m. on the green. Many have been here since 7 a.m., preparing for the series of auctions selling ewes, store lambs, stock rams, agricultural implements and machinery.

As the auctioneers' grey truck proceeds along the numbered pens where some 5000 Dorset horns, Suffolks, Border Leicesters and Texel Sheep pant and bleat, officials duck beneath boughs of ash, taking the bids from the assembled farmers with their flat caps and staffs. Over the loudspeakers, ewes' teeth are pronounced good and bids are called in a swift banter, while across the green on the fairground, families mill between fairings, candyfloss and sheepskin stalls, carrying icecreams and goldfish in bags.

By the end of the day, prizes have been awarded and sheep have been herded into the assembled trucks and lorries, leaving the straw-strewn green for another year. Priddy returns to its characteristic quiet — the only hilltop village on Mendip.

Not far from the village are the Priddy Circles, four Neolithic circles of circa 2500 BC, and, nearby, the Nine Round Barrows constructed in the next millenium by the Beaker Peoples. All around, are swallet holes, source of the river whose blue-green

40

waters flow through the caves at Wookey Hole, two miles away. There are some fifteen miles of explored cave passages at Wookey Hole, and beyond these lie an estimated 200 miles more of unexplored caverns and river passages. The 'Cave diver's Everest', Wookey currently holds the record for a dive of over 200 feet by Robert Parker in 1985, through passages carved out millions of years ago by the River Axe. Archaeological evidence has been found of occupation of these caves since 50,000 BC — flint, bone and wood tools, human and animal bones — and the caves are rife with legend.

In the Great Cave, is the 'Witch of Wookey', her louring silhouette mirrored in green waters, and around her the shadowy hollows where, earlier this century, a human skull and bones, the remains of a wooden stake, and a dagger were discovered. The shape of the witch is chronicled as early as 1470 by William of Worcester, and by 1694 was being referred to as 'the old Witch herself'. According to legend, the evil old hag of Wookey lived in the caves with her dog, casting spells which maimed the cattle, bewitched the maids, and afflicted the old with cramps and twitches, until one day, while she was cooking a child stolen from the village, the monk Father Bernard crept in and sprinkled her with Holy Water, turning her to stone forever.

Celia Fiennes, visiting the caves in 1697 wrote:

'They fancy one of the rocks resembles a woman with a great belly which the country people call the Witch which made this cavity underground for her enchantments; the rocks are glistering and shine like diamonds, and some you climbe over where one meetes with the congealed drops of water just like iceicles hanging down; some of the stone is white like alabaster and glisters like mettle...'

At that time, it was fashionable for ladies and gentlemen to retire to the caves for dancing, with music and wine — seventeenth century wine bottles have been discovered on the river bed by divers — and by the beginning of the eighteenth century, parties of six were being conducted round the caves by a local physician who charged half a crown for the visit, with beer and candles supplied. Defoe and Goldsmith were among visitors to Wookey Hole; artists of the Picturesque, like Michel Angelo Rooker, painted the mouth to the caves, and in 1739 the poet Alexander Pope 'took a fine and very uncommon petrefaction from Okey hole' for his Twickenham Grotto. Straw was laid on the cave floor, and stalactites were shot down by musketeers! There have even been children's parties held in the caves, by paper mill owner William Hodgkinson in the nineteenth century, with hide-and-seek, and stories woven from the weird and wonderful shapes in the cave formations, lit by candle or flaring torch.

With the arrival of the railway in the mid nineteenth century, numbers of visitors to the caves grew steadily, but it was not until 1927, after the introduction of electric light, that they were publicly opened. Today, more than 300,000 visitors a year descend 'Hell's Ladder', to the Witch's Kitchen to see the Witch of Wookey, her sleeping dog, and the vast white stalagmite which is 100,000 years old, and still growing. Electric light has brought mosses, algae, and the bright green hart's tongue fern to the caves. Around the lights are cave spiders, and in the shadows, pipistrelle and horseshoe bats.

Beyond the Witch's Kitchen, 200 feet below the surface, is the great circular chamber, up to 100 feet in diameter, which was carved by a whirlpool. Divers first penetrated beyond this chamber in 1935, and three years later, the first cave diving group in England was formed at Wookey Hole. Since then, successive generations of divers have explored the caves.

In 1948, Chamber 9 was reached, its 100 foot high walls shining with flowstone formations and red with iron-oxide. And now, divers can penetrate to Chamber 25, through partly flooded chambers from which mysterious sounds 'as of the clashing of cymbals' have long been recorded. But for visitors looking down from the railed walkways, Chamber 9 is the last in the guided tour. It is then a short walk through the exit tunnel and out past the Hyena Den, the Ice Age cavern where the teeth of over 450 hyena were found, to Wookey Hole's working paper mill.

Wookey Hole Paper Mill

There were once dozens of mills along the rivers of Mendip. Today, the Wookey Hole Paper Mill, which was, at the turn of the century, the biggest commercial paper mill in Europe, is a rare survivor, one of only two such mills in England. Nurtured by the clean waters of the Axe and the drying breezes along its valley, there has been a paper mill here since 1610. In 1848 the mill was bought by London stationer William Hodgkinson, and so began a period of rapid expansion. New mill buildings, a church, houses and a school for the papermakers' children were built by Hodgkinson. In its hey-day, the mill had fourteen working vats, employing some 200 people and turning out 35,000 sheets of paper per week. It even had its own brass band.

The mill was sold in the 1950s, following the decline of the handmade paper industry, but now papermaking at Wookey Hole has been revived as a commercial operation, using Victorian machinery, and paper for specialist artists' or stationery uses is exported all over the world.

Displays in the mill recreate the days when the paper was made from cotton rags brought in from Wells and Bristol, and shredded with knives by girls working at benches, whose job it was to cut out the hooks, buttons and whale-bone, in preparation for the rag boiler. Today, cotton is imported from the US cotton fields, and prepared for the vatman in the 'beaters', which crush and soak the

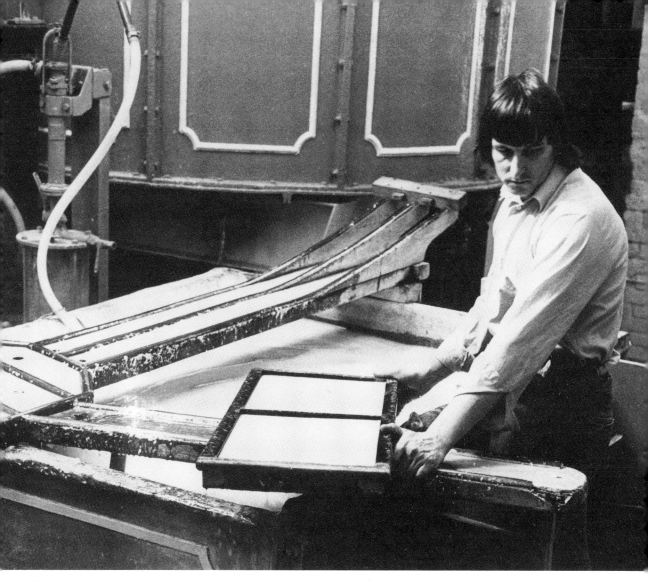

ABOVE *Papermaking at the Wookey Hole Mill*

fibres, forming a porridge-like 'stuff' of 2 per cent cotton to 98 per cent water.

Visitors to the mill can watch the rhythmic papermaking process by the vatman and his 'coucher', as the former dips and shakes the mould using his three-way 'vatman's stroke', causing the fibres to settle and weave into sheets, and the latter lays down each sheet onto a woollen felt. When a 'post' of sheets and felts has been prepared, the coucher puts them into a 140-year-old Wet Press, after which they are taken to the lofts for warm air drying from ropes of cow hair. Finally they will be pressed, and some will be glazed in the *Salle,* or Finishing Room, creating a fine cotton-based paper which will last for hundreds of years.

Beyond the mill displays, are changing exhibitions of Madame Tussaud's waxworks, and the 'Fairground by Night', a magical evocation of an Edwardian Fairground, complete with translucent lacquered figures, carved and painted gallopers, and Marenghi organs — all from Lady Bangor's collection of fairground memorabilia.

From Wookey Hole, it is a short drive to Wells, England's smallest city, nestling beneath the sheltered southern slopes of Mendip. Wells' historical division into civic and ecclesiastical quarters can still be clearly felt; the Bishop's Palace was fortified following quarrels between the Bishop and the Borough in the fourteenth century, and the ecclesiastical area of The Liberty remained free from civic jurisdiction until the 1800s. The civic life of the city centres around the Perpendicular Gothic church of St Cuthbert's — the largest parish church in Somerset — where the Medieval guilds had their chapels. This, the official church of Mayor and Corporation, with its 122 foot tower, stands at the west end of the High Street. Close by, is the City Arms Inn, the city gaol from the sixteenth to the nineteenth century, and just north of the church is the fifteenth century Guildhall, now part of Bishop Bubwith's almshouses.

It was in the fifteenth century that the market place, where markets are held every Wednesday and Saturday, emerged as the centre of Wells, when Bishop Beckington built many of the houses and provided the citizens with water from the springs in the Bishop's Palace gardens. Water still flows from the springs, via the Gothic Revival fountain which replaced the Medieval conduit, glistening and refreshing the gutters along the busy High Street of the bustling shopping centre, with its specialist shops, traditional pubs and historic eating houses. On the south side of the market place, is the Tudor Crown Inn, a timber-framed coaching inn where, a wall plaque tells us, the Quaker William Penn, the founder of Pennsylvania, preached from a window, before his arrest. Sharp-eyed visitors to Wells may also detect the brass markings in the pavement, which measure out the triumphant distance of Wells-born athlete, Mary Bignal Rand's gold medal long jump at the Tokyo Olympics.

East of the market place, two tall Medieval gateways lead us into ecclesiastical Wells. The central gate, or Bishop's Eye, takes us onto the leafy green between the Cathedral cloisters and the Bishop's Palace, where black and white tufted ducks and mute swans glide past on the Palace moat. There is a tradition that the swans have learned to ring the handbell by the drawbridge to obtain food — and visitors look on eagerly, though it would be rare to see this now.

The drawbridge leads across the moat, past the fourteenth century gatehouse, to the Medieval hall built by Bishop Jocelyn and the Bishop's tranquil gardens, where Wells' bubbling springs may be seen, and beyond, the Cathedral itself, swathed between lilac bushes and variegated foliage. The ramparts of the Bishop's Palace

44

give fine views over the surrounding Bishop's Park fields, as far as Glastonbury Tor, rising mistily on the horizon. Walkers stroll across open country within the sound of the Cathedral bells, for the tranquillity of this secluded spot may be interrupted by the exhilarating peal of the bells, or, in summer, by the sudden appearance of the Wells Morris. Dressed in white, their hats garlanded with bluebells and cow parsley, with ribbons for flamboyance and bells to ward off evil spirits, they strike the ground with their painted sticks, to rouse Nature from her winter slumber.

Their exuberance is echoed on the west front of the Cathedral, reached via the Penniless Porch where beggars used to shelter, which houses a veritable sculpture gallery of saints, kings, bishops and knights — some 296 groups beneath intricate canopies. With its spreading towers designed by William Wynford circa 1365, the west front was begun 50 years after the main body of the Cathedral, which was built from circa 1150 north of the earlier, Saxon church. Recently restored (the Prince of Wales visited Wells in June 1986 for a celebrational Eucharist) the 'poor man's bible' of the west front is one of the glories of Wells.

ABOVE *Moat of the Bishop's Palace at Wells*

ABOVE *Vicars' Close at Wells*

Inside, in the first wholly Gothic interior of an English Cathedral, the carving is focused on capitals harbouring a myriad of faces, animals and monsters. In the south transept are fruit thieves filling their baskets; a man with toothache; and east of the north porch is a farmer chasing a fox which has stolen his goose. But the most striking feature of Wells' interior is the graceful scissor arches, constructed in the fourteenth century, to counteract the thrust of the central tower, by transferring weight from the west end, where the foundations were sinking, to the firmer east end.

In the north transept is the Medieval clock, with its knights jousting every quarter, and the figure of Jack Blandiver, kicking his heels to strike the hours. Through an oak door are the famous Chapter House steps, moulded by the centuries, and leading to the thirteenth century Chapter House with its ribbed stone vault, where the business of the Chapter was conducted.

The stairs beyond lead across the covered bridge over the

Chain Gate, to the Vicars' Close, an entire street of Medieval houses built by Bishop Ralph in 1348, to house the vicars' choral. At the far end is the fifteenth century Vicars' chapel, and above it the library. From here, steps lead out into the Liberty, where the wealthy Medieval Canons lived. In this spacious area, which once belonged to Dean and Chapter are the Old Deanery, the Chancellor's House (now the Wells Museum) and, housed in Medieval and eighteenth century buildings, the Cathedral School, which dates back to the Medieval Grammar and Song School founded in the twelfth century.

South of Wells, between the Mendip and the Polden hills yet still within the Mendip District, is a still more ancient foundation — Glastonbury. In ancient times an island or peninsula rising from a vast inland lake, Glastonbury was known to the Celts as 'the Isle of Glass', and to the Saxons as 'Glastonia' — the place where woad grew. There is evidence of Prehistoric occupation of the Tor and in

Glastonbury

BELOW *King Arthur's burial place at Glastonbury Abbey*

the lake villages in the surrounding marshland, but Glastonbury's history as the 'cradle of Christianity in England', begins according to legend, in 30 AD when Joseph of Arimathea is said to have reached the Isle of Avalon with eleven disciples, on Christmas Eve. Weary of travelling, he sat down on the side of Wearyall Hill, and stuck his staff into the ground, where it sprouted, growing into the first Glastonbury Thorn. Taking this to be his sign, he built the first wattle and daub church at Glastonbury, where later England's wealthiest Abbey, and one of the finest Benedictine Houses in the country, founded by St Dunstan in the tenth century, was built.

The first great church at Glastonbury was destroyed by fire in 1184, but soon after Henry II began reconstruction, and it was then that the bodies of Arthur and Guinevere were discovered and reburied before the High Altar of the new Abbey, completed in 1524. Traditionally, the oldest and most holy part of the Abbey ruins is the Romanesque Lady Chapel, its serrated, grass-fringed ruins with their interlaced arches standing on the site of the earlier church amid daisied lawns and overlooked by Glastonbury Tor.

On this conical hill which rises 525 feet above sea level, its steep slopes still marked by the terraces of Medieval farming, pilgrims drawn by the relics of Arthur and the Celtic Saints once climbed with dry peas in their shoes. And here, after the Dissolution, the last Abbot of Glastonbury, Richard Whiting, on trial by the King's officers after the discovery of a hidden golden chalice, was executed. Today, Glastonbury pilgrims climb its steep and breezy slopes, reputed to hide a labyrinth of secret tunnels, for panoramic views over the Somerset countryside. At the summit is St Michael's Tower, the ruin of the Medieval church which replaced an earlier church built here and destroyed by earthquake in 1275.

Below, at the foot of the Tor, is the Chalice Well, or Blood Spring, set amid the clovered lawns of tranquil gardens, and connected in early Christian and Arthurian legend with the Quest for the Holy Grail, for here, it is said, Joseph of Arimathea brought the chalice of the Lord's Supper. Believed to have its source high on Mendip, the well is fed by a spring which rises on the slopes of Chalice Hill, supplying clear water even in the severest drought. Through an archway shrouded by climbing roses is the well-head, its wrought-iron lid bearing the ancient symbol of two interlocking circles, and surrounded by stone set with ammonites. From here, the water cascades down Chalice Hill, disappearing underground to emerge in a pool at the foot of the gardens, before it joins other underground streams flowing beneath the Abbey grounds. Excavations in 1961 around the well revealed the site of an ancient habitation, and the waters here have a long tradition of healing powers, though today many people come simply to enjoy the peace and tranquillity of these beautiful gardens.

RIGHT *Looking towards Mendip from the Tor at Glastonbury*

In the eighteenth century, the Chalice Well supplied the Pump Room which can still be seen on Magdalene Street. Tucked away behind it are St Margaret's Chapel and Almshouses, founded in the thirteenth century. St Margaret's, a tiny chapel with a barrel roof and fine bell cote, was built in 1270 as the chancel of the Medieval Hall Hospital of Mary Magdalene: it is said that the patients could lie in bed and see the services in the chapel, which originally opened out from the Hall. After the Dissolution, two rows of cottages were built as men's almshouses within the walls of the Great Hall. Now, only the north row remains, a favourite subject for painters, its tiny whitewashed rooms, one up one down in each house, still showing the candle holds and the cubby holes where Bibles were kept. And, through an archway beyond, on the site of the old Hospital gardens, are new homes for the elderly, sixteen modern flatlets of sheltered housing.

A short walk from St Margaret's, in the centre of Glastonbury, are further buildings of historic interest: the fifteenth century Tribunal, or court house, now a museum, where the great landowning Abbots of Glastonbury wielded their power (Glastonbury's estates stretched from Cornwall to Hampshire), and the George and Pilgrims Hotel, founded during the reign of Edward III and rebuilt in the fifteenth century by Abbot John de

BELOW *The Chalice Well at Glastonbury*

RIGHT *St Michael's Tower on Glastonbury Tor*

Selwood as an inn for pilgrims. Henry VIII is reputed to have stayed here at the time of the Dissolution, and one of the rooms — the monk's cell — is said to be haunted.

Further up the hill, one of the descendants of the Glastonbury thorn grows in the grounds of the Perpendicular church of St John the Baptist. The original Holy thorn, on Wearyall Hill, which was said to remain green all winter, was destroyed during the Commonwealth, but each year sprigs of Glastonbury thorn are cut and sent to the Queen at Christmas time.

Another thorn can be seen by the walls of St Patrick's Chapel, in the grounds of the Abbey, where visitors can also see inside the fourteenth century Abbot's kitchen, with its wood or peat fires in each corner and central lantern to ventilate the roasting oxen or the boar's head cooked for the Abbot at Christmas. The kitchen was regularly supplied with freshwater fish from Meare Pool, and today English Heritage maintains the robust stone Fish House, set amid tall grasses at Meare.

Just south of here is Street, headquarters of Britain's largest shoe manufacturers, Clarks Limited, and the southernmost town in the Mendip District. Somerset, especially the Vale of Avalon, has been famous for centuries for its sheepskin products, and the town of Street has a long history as a tanning centre for the manufacture of sheepskin rugs and footwear.

Street
Clarks Shoemaking

The Clarks, a Quaker family of yeoman farmers, came here in 1723, beginning the industry which was to make their name famous worldwide, as tanners, fellmongers and rugmakers. In 1828, the brothers Cyrus and James Clark formed a partnership, concentrating at first on sheepskin rugs, before branching out into shoemaking, with James' design for a pair of classic gentlemen's slippers — the Brown Petersburgh. Shoemaking was then a cottage industry, with outworkers bringing in their completed work every week, and collecting a new batch of soles and uppers with their pay. But under the Quaker principles of temperance and hard work, production rose dramatically in the first twenty years, and when the business suffered financial crises in 1843 and again in 1863, Clarks' Quaker friends came to their aid.

By now, the introduction of the sewing machine — with a special model for the shoemaker launched in 1863 — was boosting production, beginning a period of expansion for the business, and for the town. Many of the characteristic, Tudor-style shops and terraces in Street were built by the Clarks for their workers in the late nineteenth century. The school, now a health centre, was begun in 1913 by William Stephens Clark, who had earlier rebuilt the ale and cider house on the High Street as a coffee house — now the Bear Hotel — following in the footsteps of Cyrus and James Clark, who were strong supporters of the Temperance Movement.

FAR LEFT *The George and Pilgrims Hotel, Glastonbury*

53

LEFT *The Abbot's Kitchen at Glastonbury*

ABOVE *the Abbey's Fish House at Meare*

ABOVE *At work in Clarks Factory at Street*

It is said that the contents of Cyrus's cellar were used to mix the mortar for James' new house Netherleigh!

By 1903, when Clarks became a limited company, shoemaking had transformed Street, once a small settlement dependent on agriculture and the quarrying of the local blue lias limestone, into a thriving town. Today, the Street factory, one of ten in the Westcountry alone, specialises in children's shoes, and has some 1,700 employees, manufacturing one million pairs of shoes a year.

This is also the site of Clarks' Shoe Museum, open from May to October, which relates the history of the shoemaking industry through displays of shoes, show cards and machinery – the latter housed in the oldest part of the factory, built by Cyrus Clark in 1829 for the manufacture of rugs, mops and chamois leather from sheepskin. There are some 1,200 shoes on show here — from Roman carbatina to ladies' shoes of the seventeenth century in ruby satin and lace, or elaborate silk damask, with gold or diamond buckles. There are shoes from other countries: Russian slippers, North American moccasins, Chinese silk shoes for bound feet,

Danish house shoes made from plaited rushes. Shoes, it appears, have been made from hide, calf, kid, crocodile, snake, lizard, and even, in war-time, fish skin — with wooden soles. There is a pair of size 19 boots worn by William Legg or 'Canterbury', a 32-stone giant, 7 feet 4 inches tall, who worked on the Somerset and Dorset railway. And here is the largest boot in the world — 3 feet 8 inches high, 4 feet 3 inches long, and weighing over 81 pounds, made at Newark, in Nottinghamshire, in 1887 by John Mills & Sons, to celebrate Queen Victoria's Golden Jubilee.

The museum also recreates the type of out-workers backshop, set over the scullery, survivors of which can still be seen in Street's Orchard Road. There are still outworkers in and around the town, who stitch slippers, gloves and coats at home, as cottage workers did when Clarks began. And although the company now has a turnover of some £600 million a year, and employs 23,000 people worldwide, with factories in three continents, and shops in five countries, it remains a family firm. The present chairman, Daniel Clark is a descendant of James, while many Street families have worked in the factory for generations, and all staff are on first-name terms.

Over in Shepton Mallet, 'gateway to the Mendip Hills', another family firm, Showerings Ltd, now part of the Wine and Spirits division of Allied Lyons Ltd, became famous in the 1950s, with the launch of their naturally sparkling perry — Babycham. The Showering family has lived in Shepton Mallet since the seventeenth century, starting off here as shoemakers and innkeepers. The company was founded in 1932, by the four brothers Herbert, Arthur, Ralph and Francis who at first concentrated on brewing and cider-making until, in the 1940s, Francis began researching into the fermentation of fruit juices. By 1949, he had produced the clear naturally sparkling perry, which was launched in 1953 as Babycham — making the company's name, and fortune, virtually overnight.

Today, Showerings Ltd has diversified, producing several of the leading brands of cider, as well as new apple and perry based drinks such as Zapple, and Calviere, but 40,000 dozen bottles of Babycham are still produced here daily, using the 'double fermentation' process invented by Francis Showering.

The company owns hundreds of acres of perry pear orchards, and harvesting begins in September, when the pears are shaken from the trees by mechanical shakers and gathered in harvesters, before transport by Showering lorries to the water troughs at the factory. After washing and rinsing, the fruit is stored in one of the factory's eight 25-tonne hoppers, before passing into the hammer mill where it is chopped and prepared for processing by the giant Swiss presses. These remove the 'pomace' for cattle feed, sending only the pure fruit juice on for fermentation, or for evaporation and

ABOVE *Checking the production line at Showerings in Shepton Mallet*

storage as concentrate. It is the 'double fermentation' process, making use of the natural sugar in the juice, which produces the 'natural sparkle' in Babycham. When this is completed, the perry is piped through to the bottling lines, where some 1,920 bottles of Babycham are filled, sealed and labelled per minute, after which they are packed and loaded for distribution to pubs, clubs and shops throughout the country, and overseas.

Cider is also now produced at the Shepton Mallet factory, using apples with names like 'Fox Whelp', 'Lady's Finger', and 'Slack-ma-Girdle', combined with the juice of Bramley seedlings.

Several days a year, the public is invited in to see the Showering Gardens, which were laid out from 1960-61 under the supervision of Francis Showering. Hundreds of tons of rock from the Forest of Dean were brought in by Showering lorries to make the pathways, rockeries and waterfalls, transforming a swampy area known as the Wilderness into seven acres of landscaped grounds, where moorhens nest by the lake, and over 500 species of flowers, shrubs and trees flourish. The gardens are dominated by the towering spans of the Victorian viaduct, bought by Showerings for £5 in 1970, after the Somerset and Dorset railway was axed. And surveying all is a bronze Babycham — Showerings keep a small herd of the gentle Chinese water deer, on which their mascot is modelled, at Shepton Mallet.

In the town centre, is the new Arts and Cultural Centre built by Showerings, standing cheek by jowl with the historic heart of the town, with its ancient market cross, built around 1500 — scene of hangings, rioting, preaching, wrestling, even wife sales — and a surviving section of the Shambles, the covered Medieval market benches.

A busy market town and tourist centre today, with a population of over 7,000, 'Sheep town' developed with the wool industry: wealthy clothiers enriched the splendid church of St Peter and St Paul with its fourteenth-century tower, the earliest of the Somerset group, and later, financed by the cloth mills along the Sheppey, built many of Shepton Mallet's finer Georgian houses. Some of the old silk mills may still be seen here, at Bowlish and at Darshill.

The church tower gives panoramic views over the town, which from here looks almost continental with its narrow stone-paved alleys, grey stone walls and red pantiled rooftops. Inside, the church has a fine, timber waggon roof, framed by angels and bearing some 350 carved panels, 306 bosses and 90 half bosses — each one unique. A building of very different interest historically is Shepton Mallet's Gaol, whose high stone walls dominate the winding alleyways skirting the centre and harbour legends of mysterious hauntings.

BELOW *Showerings Warehouse at Shepton Mallet*

ABOVE *View over Shepton Mallet*

RIGHT *The gardens at Showerings*

FAR RIGHT *Looking from the tower of St Peter and St Paul at Shepton Mallet*

60

Frome

With the Mid Somerset Show and the Royal Bath and West held here annually, the town retains strong agricultural links, and the same is true of Frome, a thriving and picturesque market town situated on the eastern fringes of Mendip. With a population of over 15,000, Frome is the largest town in the Mendip District, yet the centre retains a pleasing intimacy, with charming vistas and 'roofscapes' unfolding at every turn.

One route into the town is via the steep and cobbled Gentle Street, whose gabled stone houses wind down to the church of St John the Baptist, with its golden cockerel weather-vane, and terraced churchyard. Though largely rebuilt in the nineteenth century, the church was begun circa 1100, on the site of the monastery founded by St Aldhelm on the banks of the River Frome in 685 AD. Outside, a nineteenth century *Via Crucis* depicts in stone six incidents on Christ's Way to the Cross, with the Crucifixion above the north porch. Inside, in the Lady Chapel, is the cadaver tomb of Edmund Leversedge, portraying his emaciated body lying in a shroud. The story is that he had lived a life of sin, but when his body was being carried to the Leversedge vault in the church, by torchlight, to avoid the anger of the townspeople, he suddenly came out of his coma and back to life — saying that he had seen both Heaven and Hell, and vowing to live an altered life to the end of his days.

St John's steps lead down the hill to Cheap Street, a charming, paved street lined with timber-framed shops and refreshed by a central leat. Here, the Settle tearooms serve one of Frome's specialities — Frome Bobbins, made from fruits steeped in cider and baked in light pastry whirls. Cheap Street is at the heart of the oldest part of the town which, like Shepton Mallet, grew from the fourteenth century onwards, with the cloth trade — it is said that in the days before the Crimean War, the breeches worn by the Czar's Imperial bodyguard were always made of Frome cloth, woven from handspun yarn.

The river, which winds through the lower part of the town, and once supplied the dye houses and finishing mills, is spanned by a graceful Regency bridge. Close-by is the Blue House, built in the 1720s as a combined charity school and women's almshouse, and now restored and modernised for old people's flatlets.

Across the street from here is Frome's busy market place, where every Wednesday the Cattle Market is held, in sheds alongside the market stalls. These are noisy and convivial gatherings, the sales announced by a jangling handbell, and presided over by the auctioneer, whose quick banter — 'at 450 and I'm waiting at 500 come on 500 you'll regret it' — is matched by brisk and hardly detectable bids of raised eyes and surreptitious nods.

ABOVE RIGHT *The Via Crucis, St John's Church, Frome*

BELOW *Cheap Street at Frome*

OVERLEAF *Reaching for the sky on Mendip*

Mendip:
Traditional Skills
and Crafts

Cheese Making

On the third Wednesday in September, Frome is the setting for the Cheese Show. Somerset cheeses are mentioned in records going back to the reign of Henry II — Camden's *Britannia* refers to Cheddar as 'famous for the excellent and prodigious great cheeses made there, some of which require more than a man's strength to set them on the table, and are of a delicate taste, equalling, if not exceeding that of the Parmesan.' There are stories of the caves — with their constant cool and damp atmosphere of 11 degrees centigrade — having been used as cheese stores, while many Mendip farmhouses still have their cheese rooms. Here, cheeses matured in the days when the farmer's wife and her dairy maid made one or two cheeses a day from March through to September to store the goodness of the milk for the winter months. And today, there are still farms on and around Mendip where visitors may watch the traditional 'cheddaring' process.

At Green's Farm, West Pennard, Paul Green is one of a third generation of cheese makers — his grandmother, now aged 85, trained at Cannington, and used to make the cheeses on neighbouring farms during the summer months. Today, experienced cheese maker Dave Higdon and his three assistants make fifty 60-pound cheeses a day at Green's Farm, six days a week throughout the year. Visitors are invited to ring to make an appointment to come and watch the farmhouse cheddar being made — though Dave may start the five-hour process as early as 4 a.m.!

The milk from 700 Friesians is first pumped from the road tanks into the holding tanks, where it is pasteurised at 160 degrees Fahrenheit. From here, it passes into a vat, where the starter and rennet are added, and the milk is scalded or cooked at just over 100 degrees Fahrenheit, allowing the 'junket' to rise to the top. Blades cut and stir the curds and whey, before they are transferred to the cooler or cheddaring pan, where the whey is drained off — and tested for acidity — leaving the crumbs of curd. Next comes the cheddaring process, as the cheesemakers stack, cut, pull and roll the curds, preparing the cheese for the chip mill, where it is

shredded and seasoned with salt before being packed into the moulds and put into the presses. At this stage, the rind is formed by bathing and 'grease bonding' the cheeses, using muslin dipped in lard and warm water, before they are stored, at a constant temperature of 10 degrees centigrade for up to twelve months. The 'truckles', or smaller cheeses weighing between four and eight pounds and popular for the Christmas market, are kept for only six months. At Green's Farm, cheeses are kept in the farm store for the first two months, after which they are tested by a grader, who is looking for creamy colour, waxy texture, aroma and flavour, before they are sent on to Mendip Foods.

At the Chewton Cheese Dairy, Priory Farm, Chewton Mendip, there may be up to 10,000 cheeses in the cheese store. Here, on the farm owned by Viscount Chewton, heir to the Earl Waldegrave, whose family has owned land here since the sixteenth century, they make up to a ton of traditional cheese every day, mostly cheddar, using milk from some 800 Friesians and Ayrshires on the farms at Chewton Mendip. Visitors are admitted in groups to watch the cheese-making, and across the courtyard is the farm shop, where they may buy a variety of local produce, including Mendip cheeses – and wines.

Wine Making

Somerset vineyards are recorded in the Domesday book, and following the renaissance of viniculture which began in England in the 1950s there are now some 120 vineyards in the South-West about a dozen on Somerset soil — a third producing wine professionally. Some of the vineyards on and around Mendip may be visited by appointment, including those at Whatley, Wootton, and at Pilton, just south of Shepton Mallet, where the well-drained, south-facing slopes were first planted by the monks of Glastonbury, as the Manor, which dates back to the thirteenth century, was one of five owned by the Abbey.

Vigneron Nigel de Marsac Godden came here in the 1960s — 'It was a new era, everyone was trying something different' — producing his first hogshead of Pilton Manor wine in 1967. He has now successfully cultivated some six and a half acres on Pilton soil, which is marl overlying limestone on clay and blue lias. The main varieties of grape used are a Muller Thurgau, producing a pale, delicately flavoured, medium dry white wine, and a Seyval Blanc, which gives a fresh, light dry white wine.

Every year, the vines are pruned in January and February, then

ABOVE *Pilton Manor, one of Somerset's wine producing centres* fertilised in March, and sprayed. Harvesting begins in mid October — 'always an exciting time, the culmination of a year's work', when help is enlisted from the village, the grape pickers working in pairs on either side of the rows, loading the grapes into bins ready for the trailer.

Before going into the presses, the grapes are first milled, to break the skin and free the juices. Once pressed, the juice is pumped into the fermenting tanks, where fermentation will begin after 48 hours, though the sediment must first be removed and the juice passed to a clean tank, where its acidity and sugar levels are tested, and the cultured yeast is added. Pilton Manor wine spends five months fermenting before it is bottled in the estate winery, again with the help of the villagers, in March. It is a young wine, enjoyed when it is two to four years old, with a fresh, clean taste which makes it ideal as an aperitif, or to complement white meat and fish dishes.

Soil type, altitude, the interpretation of the vigneron and the season, all contribute to the final wine, and with the English climate, the production per acre can fluctuate greatly from year to year.

'People always think the hot summer of '76 must have been our best vintage,' Nigel de Marsac Godden remarks, 'but in fact it was 1975, when the autumn perfected the *veraison,* or colour change, in the grapes. Ripening takes place in the last weeks before harvesting, and if the leaves are left on that little bit longer, it can make all the difference to the sugar and acidity levels of the final wine.'

But it is, he argues, our seasons which give the wine the essential Englishness of its character. 'It's like English peaches...the Peregrine, or the Rochester, or the Cox's Orange Pippin apple. The fruits here have to fight...they are slow to ripen, and the final taste is subtle, light, fresh...' He loves the outdoor life of the vigneron, the sense of the changing seasons, and the curious combination of agriculture, technology — and the vigneron's art. 'I find it creative...one is making something from a natural product, and always striving to create the impossible — the perfect wine.'

Like the skills of the vigneron, the craft of the basket maker has been practised in Somerset for centuries. South of the Mendips are the low-lying Somerset levels, where the withies grow, in rows two feet apart, planted out in March, and cut in November. Basket maker Alf Brewer, who demonstrates this ancient art at Glastonbury's Museum of Rural Life, grew up among the withy sets, in Stoke St Gregory, and remembers the days when the whole village helped in stripping the withies.

He was taught his craft by chairmaker Albert Champion, and now works from his home in Ashcott near Glastonbury, making baskets for his shop and to commission for distribution all over the

Basket Maker

country: cradles, picnic baskets, linen baskets, trugs, fishing creels, and the traditional 'peck' baskets, designed to hold twenty pounds of farm or garden produce.

ABOVE *Thatcher Geoff Dredge at work*

Alf has made baskets for everything, from flowers for a Lord Mayor's banquet and props for Granada television, to an Irish wolfhound, whose owner commissioned a basket 2 feet 6 inches wide and 5 feet long! He was even asked to make a vast log basket, 5 feet high and so wide that he had to make it *outside* the shed where he spends his days, quietly working with his knife, bodkin and secateurs, bending and weaving the buff, white and brown withies into shape. Alf works with the Blackmole willow, of which there are some 200 species, using lengths from three to twelve feet, of varying thickness. Linen baskets are made from the finer white (peeled) withies, heavier baskets such as trugs or pecks from the buff (boiled) withies, and/or the dark brown withies which have been steamed in the boiler with their bark still on. Patterning is introduced by following the chessboard method, or 'slewing', using more than one type of withy.

Here, Alf is working on an oval basket, with the wale (bottom border) and upsett in white, using the natural curve of the withies to start the shape.

'No two baskets are alike,' he says — and Alf should know, for he works up to twelve hours a day, basket-making in the shed at the foot of his garden, surrounded by bundles of Somerset withies.

FAR LEFT *Basket maker Alf Brewer working on an oval basket*

Thatcher

Saddler

Stone Carver

Alf works by touch, a skill important for craftsmen working in materials as diverse as leather, wood, stone — and reed. Thatcher Geoff Dredge trained locally with a master thatcher, and has spent five years thatching in the Mendip area, using Somerset reeded straw. Saddler Elisabeth Steadman, who trained at the Cordwainers' Technical College, Hackney, now runs her own saddlery at Evercreech, making and repairing saddles and top quality bridlework for a regular clientele from the Mendip hunt and pony clubs.

Directly across the Mendips, in Kilmersdon, stone and wood carver Mel Morris Jones has his workshop in the old Wesleyan chapel by the church. Mel trained in London and was head carver at Westminster Abbey before moving to the Mendips, where today he undertakes a variety of commissions, many using locally quarried stone such as Portland, Bath, Doulting and Lepine stone. His previous commissions have included corinthian capitals for St Paul's churchyard, a dolphin group after Wren, for the Royal Naval College, Greenwich, and a *Majesta* or Christ in Majesty for the Bishop of Southwark. And today, his work may be seen on Mendip — in one of the proud dogs guarding the gateposts of Chewton House, and in some of the stiff-leaved capitals adorning the restored west front of Wells Cathedral.

ABOVE *Stone and wood carver Mel Morris Jones*

Inside the cathedral are new pipe shades for the organ, carved in wood by another Mendip craftsman, wood turner and designer Ray Holloway, who was apprenticed to a joiner in the ecclesiastical trade, and now has his own workshop at Draycott, near Cheddar. Ray works in woods such as lime, oak, beech and mahogany, undertaking ecclesiastical and secular commissions, from the rood screen for Crewkerne Church, to windows for King John's Hunting Lodge, Axbridge. Here, he is seen working on one of the barley-twist balustrades for a copy of a Georgian staircase in Cuban mahogany inlaid with oak, for a house in Queen Square, Bath.

Visitors to the Pump Room in Bath may have heard the Bath Georgian Festival Society, or the London Bach Orchestra, playing one of the harpsichords made by Christopher Barlow. Born in Birmingham and trained at King Alfred's, Winchester, Christopher now works as a musical instrument maker from his workshop at the Welsh Mill, Frome. Working from measured drawings, in specially supplied woods such as sitka spruce or pine for the sound boards, with ebony, boxwood, pearwood and holly for detail, Christopher designs, copies and repairs instruments for patrons in this country and as far afield as Australia and the United States.

Wood Turner and Carver

Musical Instrument Maker

BELOW *Wood carver Ray Holloway*

In his workshop at the Welsh Mill is a square piano of 1825, which someone had turned into a desk, a Grecian double action harp by Sebastian Erard, which he found in a junk shop, and the minstrel harp he made in black walnut as a college apprentice piece. Since then, he has made diverse instruments, from an 'Appalachian dulcima' and an Aeolian 'zither' or harp in yew, to a copy of Pascal Taskin's double manual harpsichord of 1769. Working with precision to one tenth of a millimetre, detail such as turning pins and stop levers are exactly copied, though Christopher may use modern materials such as steel for strength and durability, in combination with traditional materials such as leather for a register, pearwood jacks, and boxwood heads to the ebony keys.

Signwriter

Another craftsman, who works both to his own designs and on copies of earlier work, is signwriter Andrew Goldsworthy, whose inn signs may be seen on and around Mendip, as at the Sherston Inn, just down the road from his Wells workshop. Trained at art school in Taunton, Andrew settled in Somerset in the early 1970s, having previously travelled as a showman's artist, painting fairground gallopers. Today, he works both for the local trade, and for the major breweries, painting inn signs, murals and facsimile signs, using oil or oil-based paints and signwriters' enamel paints. Here he is transferring a design using templates for a copy of the Somerset Guild of Craftsmen's sign, for St Margaret's, Taunton.

Artist

Across the hills from Wells at Rickford, near the bottom of Blagdon Coombe, is the Mendip Painting Centre, run by David and Rosalind Cuthbert and founded in 1971 by artist Peter Coate, RWA. Born in Nailsea, Peter trained at the Chelsea School of Art, London, and has exhibited in London and Bristol as well as at the West of England Academy and at his home in Ston Allerton. Mendip is, he says, 'a marvellous area for painting. I like the wildness and solitude, the austerity; painting a mile away from any road, where I might only see one person on the skyline all day.' He paints the old limekilns, the dewponds, the rocks — enjoying above all Mendip's craggy rock faces and weathered outcrops of limestone. 'I love the rocks of Mendip...limestone rocks are very beautiful in shape, texture and the subtlety of their colours.'

He has also embarked on a series of Mendip churches, beginning with the west front of Wells and a print of his painting went on sale for the Cathedral appeal. Here, he enjoys not only the draughtsmanship of line and angle, but the church settings, amid ancient yews and weathered tombstones. 'Best of all I like painting the remote churches, like Chewton Mendip.'

Often, Peter will spend all day at some remote spot, high above the Cheddar Gorge, and he admits that he has to be hardy, though for painting he positively enjoys bad weather. Winter, he says, 'brings out the skeleton of things. The more unpredictable the

FAR RIGHT *Musical instrument maker Christopher Barlow*

74

weather is, the better it is for painting. I like the challenge of a sky that is not going to be the same for a minute.' He has even found himself half way down a cliff face in a gale, everything pitted against him, in the pursuit of his art.

In many of his paintings, there is a sense of transience, the urgency of something passing away — the corn about to be cut, a decaying limekiln, a passing raincloud or approaching snowstorm. He will often paint the same subject again and again, in different lights and moods, and with its meadows, copses, streams, commanding views and rugged hills, Mendip offers as wide a variety for the painter as it does for the walker or rider.

BELOW *Peter Coate with some of his paintings of Mendip rocks*

76

ABOVE *Sign painter Andrew Goldsworthy*

Places of Interest:
Some Mendip Buildings

Fishing

At Blagdon, the scenery and the tranquillity are enjoyed by another group of enthusiasts, anglers like Ron Neil and Malcolm Charsley. Malcolm has been a regular angler at the Blagdon and Chew Valley Reservoirs for the past ten years, fishing seven days a week whenever he can. The season runs from April to October, and on summer days he may be out for over twelve hours, setting out in his boat at 10 a.m., and coming back for the weigh-in an hour after sunset. Like Malcolm, Ron Neil has been fishing since he was a boy, and he now works as a part-time warden at Blagdon Lodge. Ron has been fishing all over the world, and has caught marlin in the Indian Ocean, but he would not swop Blagdon, with its two-mile-long lake surrounded by wooded slopes, for anywhere.

Blagdon Reservoir

'Cradle of reservoir fishing in Britain', Blagdon was opened in 1904 and is now renowned as a fine trout lake, with over 16,000 fish caught during the 1985 season, weighing an average of 1 pound 15 ounces. At the lodge where Ron works is the biggest fish ever landed from Blagdon's banks: a 16 pound 5 ounce rainbow trout

RIGHT *Chew Valley Reservoir*

FAR RIGHT *Malcolm Charsley at Chew Valley*

78

ABOVE *Gate posts to the carriage drive at Cranmore Hall, now All Hallows School*

Chew Valley Reservoir

Cheddar Reservoir

caught in 1986, and here too, above the mantelpiece, is a brace of brown trout caught during Blagdon's first season, back in September 1904. For Ron, it is the 'sense of anticipation' which makes fishing at Blagdon exciting, and he, like Malcolm, enjoys the peace and quiet and the beauty of the lake, especially in the early morning or late evening, when the flies begin to hatch out and the air is thick with swallows, swifts and martins.

The Chew Valley lake, too with its natural feature of Denny island, is a 'fisherman's paradise', with a reputation for offering the finest lake trout fishing in Europe. Opened by the Queen in 1956, Chew Valley is one of the largest artificial lakes in the South West, with some 4500 million gallons of water covering 1200 acres; rainbow trout weighing more than thirteen pounds have been caught here. At the southern end, around Herriott's Bridge, is a Nature Reserve, where over 200 species of birds, resident and migrant have been recorded, including a small flock of Bewick swans. This is an important inland water for wintering wild fowl, and some 4000 birds are ringed annually by the Ringing Station opened in 1963, and run by the British Trust for Ornithology.

As at Cheddar Reservoir, which offers coarse fishing, there is sailing and windsurfing at Chew Valley lake, and in the summer months, its picturesque banks are a popular place for families to while away the hours, watching the colourful sails criss-crossing on the water.

Another popular place for families and enthusiasts alike, is the East Somerset Railway at Cranmore, founded in 1975 by its chairman, wildlife artist David Shepherd. The original East Somerset railway, opened as a broad gauge railway in 1858, ran from Witham via Cranmore to Shepton Mallet, on the picturesque Cheddar Valley, or 'Strawberry Line', and today, steam-hauled passenger trains are running again from Cranmore to Merryfield Lane, and out into the picturesque Mendip Vale, giving views over the Somerset countryside to Shepton Mallet and beyond.

From April to October, on Sundays, public holidays and certain Wednesdays and Saturdays, visitors can travel on locomotives such as the Green Knight, the 140-ton Black Prince, and the diminutive Lord Fisher, or can watch from the station platform, which in every detail, from the white picket fencing to the railway posters and station name boards, recalls the Age of Steam.

The station building at Cranmore is the original (dating from 1858) as is the cast iron 'Gents' on the platform, and along the line, a 130-foot-long, Victorian-style steam depot, with a traditional locomotive coaling stage outside has been built, recreating the 'cathedral atmosphere' of the great steam sheds. Across the track, the once-derelict signal box has been restored and converted into the Signal Box Art Gallery, with David Shepherd's wildlife, steam

East Somerset Railway

BELOW *The East Somerset Railway at Cranmore*

railway and landscape prints on sale upstairs, and downstairs a museum of railway relics.

Another, more recently restored attraction at Cranmore is the 150 foot Cranmore Tower, standing 953 feet above sea level amid fifty acres of woodland in the Mendip Forest. The tower was built in 1862 in the Italianate style by James Wyatt for the Paget family of Cranmore Hall — now All Hallows School — who had their shooting lodge, and held picnic parties here. Until recently, the tower was under threat of collapse, but it has now been restored by Donald and Kate Beaton, who had seen it 'crumbling away' on their walks through Cranmore Wood. Visitors can climb the 182 steps to enjoy one of the finest views in Somerset, extending on a clear day, Donald says, over six counties.

It is no longer possible to climb the rival Ammerdown Tower in the parish of Kilmersdon, north of Cranmore, but the column remains an impressive landmark, set amid fields of corn high above Ammerdown House, its glass dome 700 feet above sea level. The column was begun in 1885 by Colonel Joliffe as a memorial to his father, Thomas Samuel Joliffe, who built Ammerdown House in the late eighteenth century, laid out the wooded park and improved much of the land here for grazing and cultivation.

The mansion, set amid formal gardens designed by Lutyens, remains a private house, while many of Mendip's larger houses have adapted to new roles, as at Ston Easton, seat of the Hippisley family since the sixteenth century, where the eighteenth century Palladian Manor is now a gracious hotel. Inside, is some of the finest Georgian decoration in the west of England. The saloon, with its *grisaille* panels, Corinthian columns and ornate ceiling, has been described as 'the finest room in Somerset'. Its windows look north over the sloping lawns, wooded walks and cascading stream created by Humphrey Repton, and planned in his Red Book

Cranmore Tower

Ammerdown Tower

Ston Easton

ABOVE *Ston Easton now an hotel*

FAR LEFT *The Ammerdown Tower*

RIGHT *Oakhill Manor*

ABOVE *Gardens at Oakhill Manor*

84

of 1792-1793. Two bridges span the stream, one accommodating a sham castle folly which abuts the gardener's cottage with its rustic porch and mullioned windows. Through an archway, is a walled flower garden and the estate glass houses; elsewhere the eighteenth century parkland features wells, a ruin and an ice-house.

High on the Mendips at Oakhill Manor, built in the nineteenth century by the brewing family, the Spencers, new attractions have been introduced. The Victorian mansion now houses Walter Harper's Master Modellers' Collection, while outside a miniature railway runs through tree-shaped glades, between rocky banks and under tunnels, giving views over Oakhill's 45-acre estate, whose southern boundaries reach down to the Oakhill Brewery, founded in 1767 and famous for its Oakhill stout.

Contemporary with Oakhill Manor, is the model Victorian homestead at Eastwood Manor Farm, East Harptree, believed to have been designed by Robert Smith, and built at a cost of £15,000 by Frank Taylor, the former butler who married a Miss Gurney of Harptree Court. The steading, with its impressive Victorian Gothic façade, is designed around two flagged bullock yards, with drinking troughs watered from central fountains supplied from the Whelly stream, and roofed over with one and a half acres of glass and galvanised iron. Stabling was provided for eight three-horse teams

BELOW *Eastwood Manor Farm*

85

LEFT *Downside Abbey at Stratton on the Fosse*

ABOVE *The Roman Catholic Church, formerly a tithe barn, at Midsomer Norton*

RIGHT *The Church at Witham*

Midsomer Norton
Roman Catholic Church

Downside Abbey

of cart horses, along with the stallion, carriage and riding horses, and the homestead was equipped with its own blacksmith's and carpenter's shops, 500-ton grain store, grist and flour mills, and outside a fish hatchery, with nine trout ponds.

Today, the Eastwood Manor farm buildings remain part of the working farm run by Alfred Gay, while east of here, in Midsomer Norton, another of Mendip's historic buildings has adapted to a new role. The fifteenth century Tithe Barn once owned by the Augustinian Canons of Merton Priory, Surrey, was blessed as a Roman Catholic church in May 1913. Having passed to the Crown after the Dissolution, the barn had been put to a variety of uses, from kennels to a chicken house, until its purchase by Downside Abbey in 1906. Though the interior was restored and adapted by Giles Gilbert Scott, the three-foot thick, buttressed sandstone walls and vast doorways, designed to accommodate carts piled high with unthreshed corn, remain clues to the building's original function.

Downside Abbey and School were founded at Stratton on the Fosse, south of Midsomer Norton, in the nineteenth century, when the Benedictine Community of St Gregory the Great fled here from Douai in Flanders after the French Revolution. The Abbey's fine Neo-Gothic church, with its nave and 166 foot tower designed by Giles Gilbert Scott, developed, like the monastery and school buildings around it, in the Medieval manner, under the direction of successive architects. There are some 600 pupils, mainly boarders, at the Independent Catholic Boys' School at Downside, housed in a pleasingly eclectic mixture of buildings from the seventeenth century Old House, through the Gothic Revival wings to the modern refectories and six-storey hexagonal library.

Downside remains a living school and monastic community, while at Witham, on the eastern foothills of the Mendips, are the remains of the first Carthusian House in England. Witham Friary was founded here in the twelfth century, when Henry II gave the royal manor of Witham to the Carthusians as part of his atonement for the death of Thomas à Becket. The church, with its vaulted stone ceiling, was rebuilt as a lay brothers' chapel under Hugh of Witham, later Bishop of Lincoln, and after the Dissolution it remained as the parish church. Opposite, is the Medieval dovecote, used in the last century as the village reading room until restoration in 1910, when over 1000 doveholes were uncovered, some still containing ears of wheat. Today, the dovecote is used as a photographer's studio.

Witham Friary

Another survivor of the great monastic houses is the George Inn at Norton St Philip, one of the oldest licensed houses in the country, dating back to the early thirteenth century. The inn was originally a Carthusian hostelry, belonging to the Priory at Hinton

George Inn Norton St Philip

ABOVE *The Old Down Inn at Emborough*

Charterhouse, and its top storey was used as a wool store, for the monks were sheep breeders and wool merchants, holding wool fairs and a weekly market here. After the Dissolution, the George remained an inn; Samuel Pepys, on his way to Bath with his wife and servants in 1668 put up his horses here and 'dined very well' for ten shillings. And in the troubled days leading up to the Battle of Sedgemoor, the Duke of Monmouth is said to have narrowly missed an assassin's shot as he shaved by his window in a room at the George.

Cannard's Grave Inn

A more gruesome story lies behind the sign at the Cannard's Grave Inn, where five roads meet, south of Shepton Mallet. Giles Cannard, innkeeper here in the seventeenth century, was notorious for his underhand deals with the sheepstealers, highwaymen and smugglers who haunted the lanes roundabout. But when the townsfolk discovered his attempt to defraud them of common land, they marched on the inn, and Cannard, the story has it, hanged himself. Some say he was buried with a stake through the heart, in the inn's porch; others that his ghost still haunts the crossroads where his gang used to lie in wait for solitary travellers.

Old Down Inn, Emborough

During the mail coach era, the Old Down Inn at Emborough, standing at an important crossroads, between the A37 and the B3139, on the London-Bath-Exeter route, held its own postmark. Inland mail, as well as the packet mail from Falmouth was delivered here, for franking and delivery to neighbouring towns and villages, or despatch by the mail car to Bristol, for Wales and the north.

Like Mendip's many historic inns, the churches are

repositories of history. A walk around the churchyard reveals family names, glimpses of a village's past. At St Laurence, East Harptree, poor relief was once paid from a large flat tomb or 'pay table' in the churchyard; at Banwell is the faceless, weathered bust of William Beard, nineteenth century farmer, antiquary and pioneer cave explorer, who built the wall of bones in Banwell Cave. There are enigmas, too, like the tomb inscription of Edward Jones at Burrington, 'Born Novr ye 15th 1708 and dyed March ye 14th 1708', a chronological puzzle created by the calendar previous to 1752, which began the New Year on 25 March.

Burrington Church has some of the finest gargoyles on Mendip carved on its rich, late Perpendicular exterior. Other good examples may be seen at Kilmersdon and at St Peter's, Evercreech, where three intriguing gargoyles on the south side are said to have been carved by a stone mason from Wells who, having had a row with the vicar, the publican and two women in turn, represented them here as a monster, a monkey and two gossiping cats!

St Peter's 110 foot Perpendicular tower is renowned for its ring of ten bells, while across the hills at St Margaret's, Hinton Blewett, the tower is graced by a set of five 'Bilbie bells', the tenor bearing the inscription 'Bilbie cast all wee, 1708'. There are stories of John Bilbie, famous bell caster of Chew Stoke, sitting in his pond up to

BELOW *The George Inn at Norton St Philip*

RIGHT *Stained glass window at Banwell church illustrating the miracle of the baby in the bath*

his ears in water, while his assistants banged the newly cast bells hanging in a wooden frame close by; this, it is said, was the way he tested how the bells would sound from the tower. Hinton Blewett has a long tradition of bell ringing, both in the church, and by the teams of hand-bell ringers who used to call at farms and houses in the Chew Valley to ring in the New Year, and today a team of eight regular ringers at the church maintains the tradition.

Though St Margaret's is a Perpendicular church, its tower was rebuilt in the eighteenth century, but just south of here, at Chewton Mendip, is one of the finest Perpendicular towers in Somerset. The 126 foot tower of St Mary Magdalene was begun circa 1440, and took 100 years to complete — in 1535 Leland commented on the 'goodly new high tourred steple of Chewton Mendip'.

Another fine Perpendicular church, St Andrew's at Banwell, has been called 'the Cathedral of the Mendips'. Among the treasures in its rich interior are the panels of Medieval glass in the east windows of the aisles, one representing the miraculous preservation of a child's life during his mother's absence at the consecration of St Nicolas as Bishop of Myra: she had left her baby in a bath over the fire, and returned to find the water boiling!

Banwell church also has a fine chancel screen, intricately carved with vineleaves and dating from 1521, while St Mary the Virgin at Croscombe contains some of the finest Jacobean woodwork in the country. Set on a steep hill giving views over the red pantiled rooftops of Croscombe to the green valley sides, the church itself dates from the fifteenth century, and the dark rose bosses on its richly carved waggon roof bear symbols of the clothiers' trade. But much of the interior was embellished during

LEFT *The Latch Monument at St John the Baptist Church, Churchill*

the seventeenth century: the elaborate carved pulpit and canopy given by Bishop Lake; the tall, dark oak box pews by the Fortescue family, Lords of the Manor from the early sixteenth century, whose arms, along with those of James I, adorn the screen.

The seventeenth century also produced some of the lavish, painted tombs in Mendip churches, such as the memorial to Anne Prowse in St John's, Axbridge, and the Latch Monument in St John the Baptist, Churchill. The story is that Sir John Latch, returning home after the Battle of Newbury to find his wife Sara had died in childbirth the day before, was struck dead as he looked at her corpse. He is shown beside her shrouded figure; beneath is the baby swathed in black, and the mourning figures of their eleven children, four carrying the skulls of their own deaths.

More crowded still is the frieze of mourning children — eight sons and twelve daughters — decorating the tomb of Sir John Newton, Bt, whose armour-clad effigy lies flanked by ionic

columns, beneath an ornate canopy panelled with Tudor roses, in the porch of St Laurence, East Harptree.

Its grandeur here is unexpected, as is the enchanting interior of one of Mendip's smallest, and now sadly 'redundant' churches, St James' at Camelay. There is much here of historical interest, from the Medieval pews, two-decker pulpit and Queen Anne Gallery, to the separate entrances, one leading to the pews for the gentry and farmers, the other to the gallery, for the rest. But St James' most intriguing feature is the ghosts of once-vibrant wall paintings: eleventh century masonry painting in muted earth colours, a fourteenth century figure of a jester, and red and yellow damask patterning on the fifteenth century chapel walls.

Like the tiny, Norman church at Christon, whose windows overlook Crook's Peak, St James' Camelay is one of the many, unexpected gems to be found on and around Mendip, in countryside as varied as the treasures themselves.

95

Other Bossiney Titles Include

THE QUANTOCKS
by Jillian Powell with photographs by Julia Davey
'Seen from Taunton or The Mendips, the Quantocks look timeless . . .' Sensitive combination of words and pictures produce a delightful portrait of the area.
'It is a fascinating book . . . splendidly written and with stunning photographs.'
Clinton Rogers & Polly Lloyd, BBC Bristol

PEOPLE AND PLACES IN BRISTOL
Introduced by E. V. Thompson
Five authors take a look at People and Places in Bristol.
'Words and pictures – many of them especially commissioned for this book – portray a rich Bristol heritage.'
West Review

WESTCOUNTRY MYSTERIES
Introduced by Colin Wilson
A team of authors probe mysterious happenings in Somerset, Devon and Cornwall. Drawings and photographs all add to the mysterious content.
'. . . unresolved stories from past and present. Most beguiling is David Foot's essay on Thomas Shoel, the 18th century composer from Somerset. I would buy the book for that story alone.'
Margaret Smith, Express and Echo

KING ARTHUR IN SOMERSET
by Rosemary Clinch and Michael Williams
The authors travel among the various Arthurian sites in Somerset and Avon.
'. . . leaves one not only with a better knowledge of Somerset, but also a great sense of awe for all the people who trod these hills and fields before us.'
Monica Wyatt, Chard & Ilminster News.

UNKNOWN SOMERSET
by Rosemary Clinch and Michael Williams
Spans the century in words and pictures. Featured on Channel 4.
'This is a lovely book. As you browse through the pages every picture seems to catch your eye and sends you off on a different track.'
Polly Lloyd, BBC Radio Bristol

MYSTERIES IN THE SOMERSET LANDSCAPE
by Sally Jones
Sally Jones, in her fourth Bossiney title, travels among the Mysteries in the Somerset Landscape. An intriguing journey among deep mysteries in a 'fascinating and varied landscape.'
'This is a whirlwind package holiday of sorcery and legend, touching down here and there before whizzing off in search of still more fascinating fare.'
Mid Somerset Series of Newspapers

UNKNOWN BRISTOL
by Rosemary Clinch
Introduced by David Foot, this is Bossiney's first Bristol title. 'Rosemary Clinch relishes looking round the corners and under the pavement stones . . .'
'Not a normal guide . . . it's a lovely book and very interesting . . .'
Penny Downs, BBC Radio Bristol

SUPERNATURAL IN SOMERSET
by Rosemary Clinch
Atmospheres, healing, dowsing, fork-bending and strange encounters are only some of the subjects featured inside these pages. A book, destined to entertain and enlighten – one which will trigger discussion – certain to be applauded and attacked.
'. . . an illustrated study of strange encounters and extraordinary powers . . .'
Somerset County Gazette

OFFBEAT SOMERSET
by Dan Lees
Author and journalist, Dan Lees, explores some off-beat stories and characters of Somerset.
'. . . he has looked at the story behind the story . . .'
Somerset & Avon Life

LEGENDS OF SOMERSET
by Sally Jones. 65 photographs and drawings.
Sally Jones travels across rich legendary landscapes. Words, drawings and photographs all combine to evoke a spirit of adventure.
'On the misty lands of the Somerset plain – as Sally Jones makes clear – history, legend and fantasy are inextricably mixed.'
Dan Lees, The Western Daily Press

E. V. THOMPSON'S WESTCOUNTRY
This is a memorable journey: combination of colour and black-and-white photography. Bristol to Land's End happens to be the Bossiney region, and this is precisely E. V. Thompson's Westcountry.
'Stunning photographs and fascinating facts make this an ideal book for South West tourists and residents alike – beautifully atmospheric colour shots make browsing through the pages a real delight.'
Jane Leigh, Express & Echo

We shall be pleased to send you our catalogue giving full details of our growing list of titles for Devon, Cornwall and Somerset and forthcoming publications.

If you have difficulty in obtaining our titles, write direct to Bossiney Books, Land's End, St Teath, Bodmin, Cornwall.